Contents

Some words are shown in bold, **like this**. You can find out what they mean by looking in the glossary.

 Find out more about construction toys at
www.heinemannexplore.co.uk

Construction toys

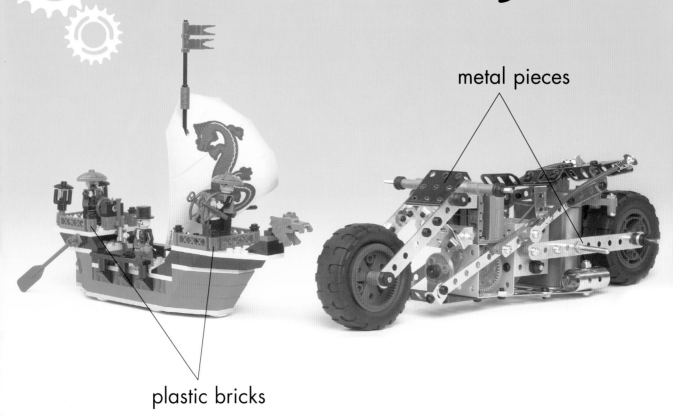

metal pieces

plastic bricks

You can make almost anything you like using **construction** toys! Some construction toys use plastic bricks. Others are made of metal and use **nuts** and **bolts** to hold them together.

Some building toys have moving parts. This giant dinosaur model was made by putting lots of smaller pieces together.

5

Building bricks

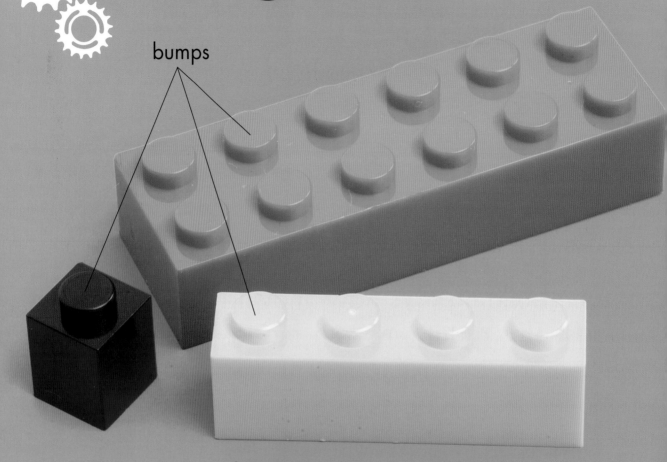

bumps

These are building bricks. They come in different shapes and sizes. All of the bricks have bumps on the top.

Bricks can be joined together to make
bigger shapes. The bumps on top of each
brick fit into the bottom of other bricks.
By putting the bricks together you can
make a strong wall or tower.

Making shapes

Bricks can be put together to make many shapes. Square and rectangular bricks can be built into a slope or triangle shape. The rows of bricks get shorter as you build higher.

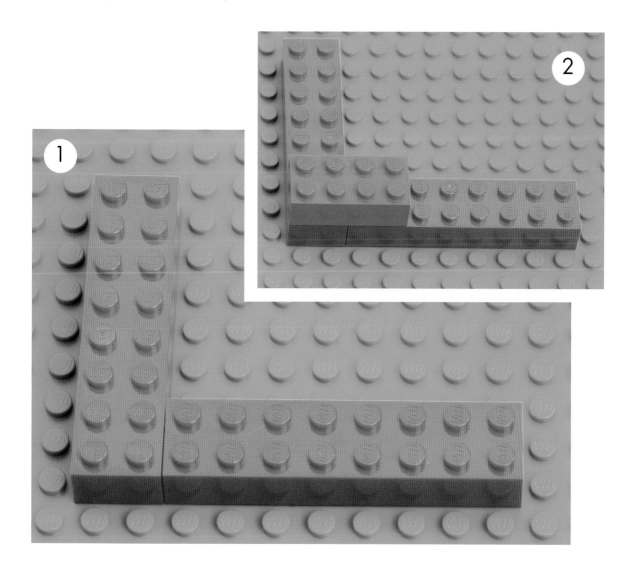

Bricks can be used to make corners.
First put two bricks together in the shape
of a letter "L". Then put another brick
over the top of them to join the two
bricks together.

Bricks that do things

brick with axle

Some bricks have moving parts. The brick on the right of this photo has an **axle** in it. You can put wheels on the axle and use the brick to make a car.

the arms move

the eyes light up

Some bricks use **electricity** to do different things. They can move, light up, or even make sounds! The bricks in this monkey toy get their electricity from **batteries**.

the battery inside the brick provides electricity

11

Making big models

You can make very big models
by using lots and lots of bricks.
To make this model you need lots
of different-shaped bricks.

This model lion uses lots of big bricks. The finished model is even bigger than a child!

Rods and connectors

connectors

rods

This toy is made of **rods** and **connectors**. Rods are long, thin poles. Connectors join things together. There are rods of different lengths. There are also different kinds of connectors.

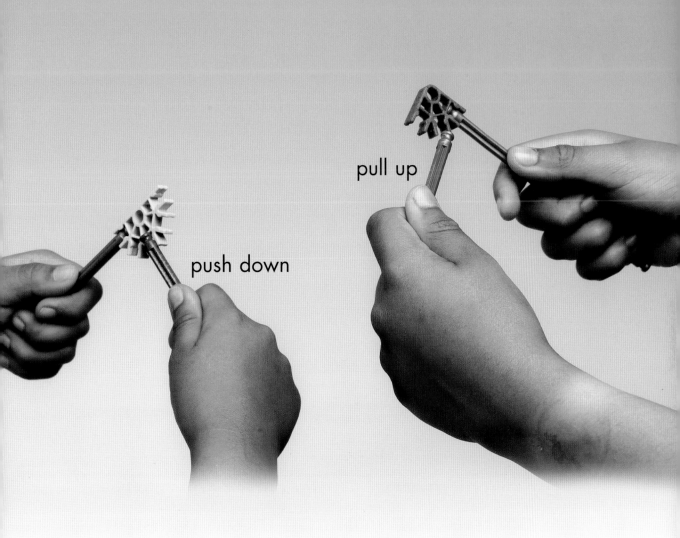

push down

pull up

You can join rods together by pushing the ends into a connector. Each rod clicks into place. You can take a rod out again by pulling it.

Making shapes with rods

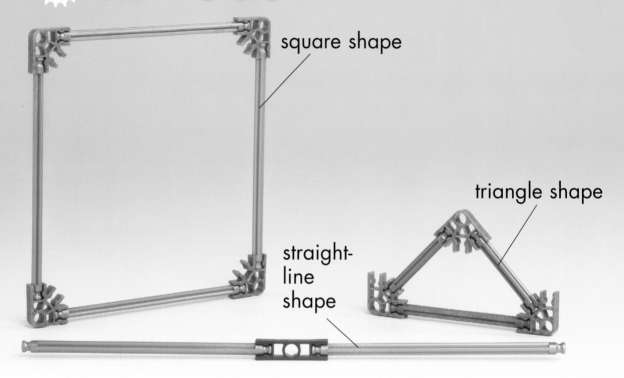

square shape

triangle shape

straight-line shape

By pushing **rods** into different parts of a **connector** you can make different shapes. These connectors have been used to make square, triangle, and straight-line shapes.

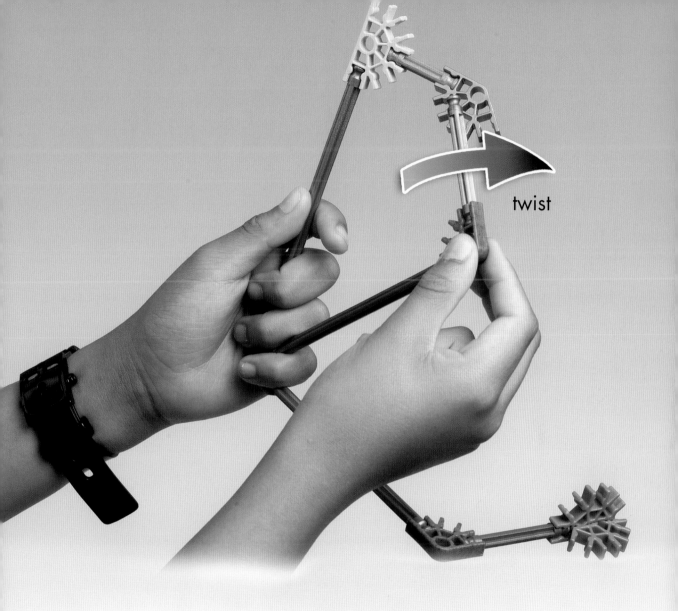

twist

You can use lots of rods and connectors to make a really big model. Sometimes you need to turn or twist the rods to make them fit together.

Models with wheels

An **axle** is a **rod** that holds a wheel and lets it turn around. The rods of this model can be used as axles. The wheels are pushed on to the rods and then built into the buggy.

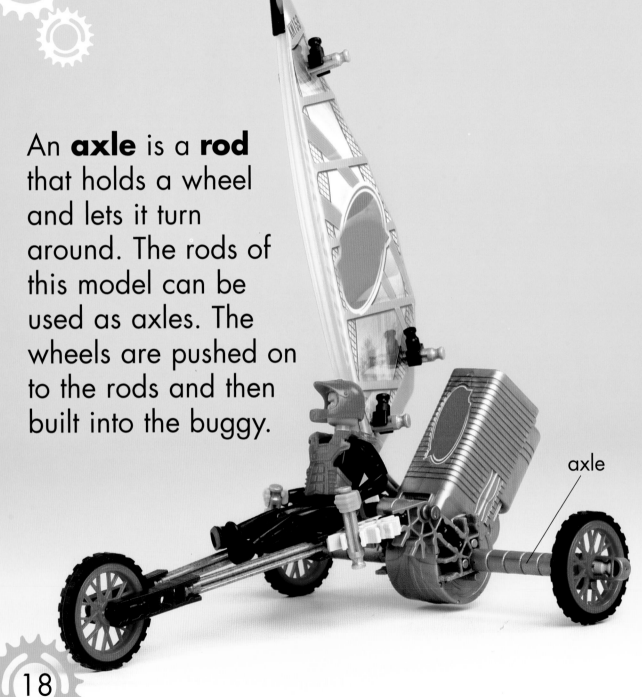

axle

wheels turn round

push

When the buggy is pushed, the wheels turn round. This means the buggy can move forwards.

How things move

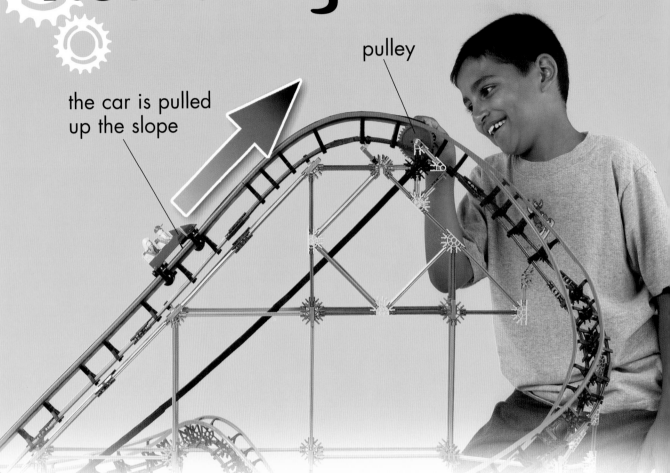

the car is pulled up the slope

pulley

A **pulley** is a wheel with string going around it. The pulley on this model roller coaster is used to pull the car up the slope. When the wheel is turned, the string lifts the car up.

gravity pulls the car down

Gravity pulls everything towards the ground. Gravity is pulling this car down the slope of the roller coaster. The car is going so fast that it will not need to be pulled up the next slope.

Connecting pieces

holes

This building toy uses metal pieces with holes in them. The holes are needed to join the pieces together.

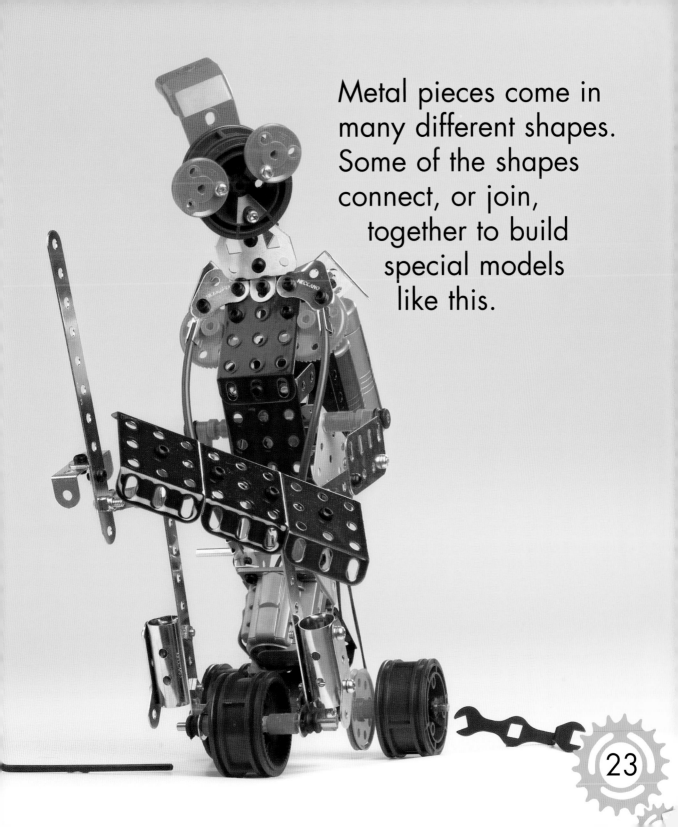

Metal pieces come in many different shapes. Some of the shapes connect, or join, together to build special models like this.

Nuts and bolts

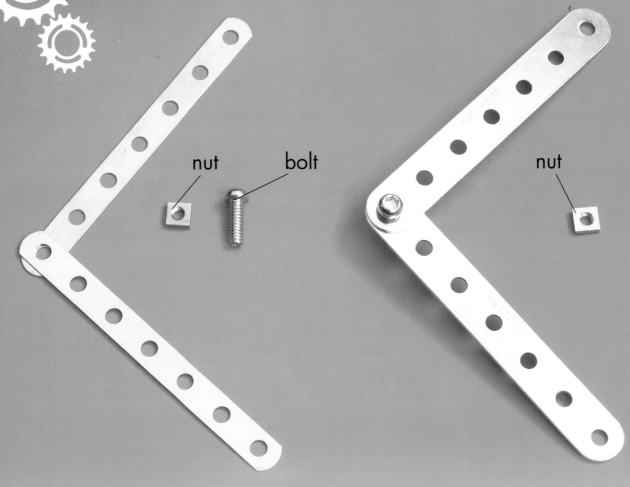

nut   bolt   nut

To join these pieces together you need a **nut** and a **bolt**. You must line up all the holes you want to join up. The bolt is the part that goes through the holes.

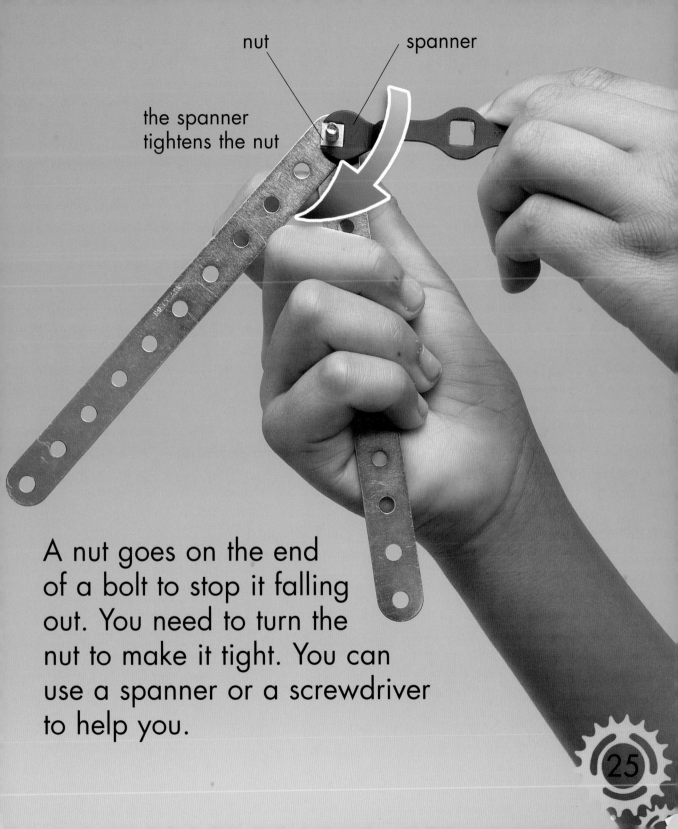

nut

spanner

the spanner
tightens the nut

A nut goes on the end
of a bolt to stop it falling
out. You need to turn the
nut to make it tight. You can
use a spanner or a screwdriver
to help you.

25

Models with motors

motor

wheels

nuts   bolts

Simple metal pieces can be put together with a **motor** to make large models that move.

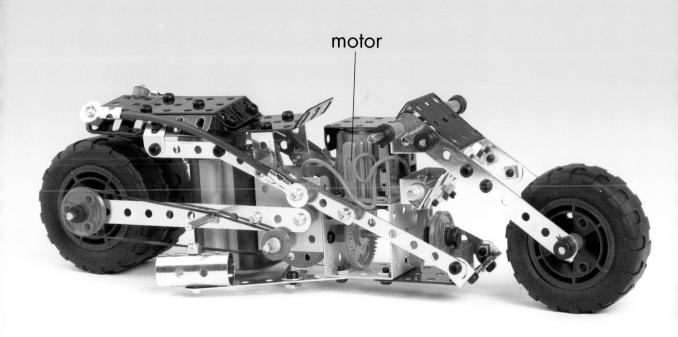

motor

This motorbike has been built using
wheels, nuts, bolts, and a motor.
The motor makes the wheels
turn and the motorbike move.

Spot the difference!

Construction toys can be used to build the most amazing things. One of these photos shows a giant model of New York, USA, made of plastic bricks. The other is a photo of the real city. Can you tell which is which?

 Find out more about construction toys at
www.heinemannexplore.co.uk

Glossary

axle rod that holds a wheel but still lets the wheel
turn around

battery something that stores electricity

bolt metal pin used to hold things together

connector shape that joins two or more rods together

construction building

electricity kind of energy used for lighting, heating,
and making machines work

gravity force that pulls everything down towards
the ground

motor something that uses electricity or fuel to make
a machine move

nut piece of metal with a hole in the middle.
It is screwed on to the end of a bolt to hold
things together.

pulley wheel used with a string, rope, or chain to
make lifting things easier

rod long, thin piece of plastic or metal

Find out more

More books to read

Building Bridges, David Glover (Longman, 2004)

LEGO Crazy Action Contraptions: A LEGO Ideas Book, Don Rathjen (Klutz Press, 1999)

Toys! Amazing Stories Behind Some Great Inventions, Don L. Wulffson (Henry Holt and Co., 2000)

Websites to visit

http://www.ericharshbarger.org/lego/portfolio.html
This website has photos of lots of amazing models made from construction bricks!

http://www.lego.com
This website has lots of games to play and ideas for great things to build with bricks.

http://www.knex.com
Sticks and rods make fantastic shapes and models on this site.

Disclaimer

All the Internet addresses (URLs) given in this book were valid at the time of going to press. However, due to the dynamic nature of the Internet, some addresses may have changed, or sites may have changed or ceased to exist since publication. While the author and Publishers regret any inconvenience this may cause readers, no responsibility for any such changes can be accepted by either the author or the Publishers.

Index